For Ruth, with love—S.L.R.

For my sisters, Julie and Susan—C.T.

PARROTS
OVER
PUERTO RICO

by **Susan L. Roth** and **Cindy Trumbore**

collages by **Susan L. Roth**

Lee & Low Books Inc. New York

Above the treetops of Puerto Rico flies a flock of parrots as green as their island home. If you look up from the forest, and you are very lucky, you might catch the bright blue flashes of their flight feathers and hear their harsh call.

These are Puerto Rican parrots. They lived on this island for millions of years, and then they nearly vanished from the earth forever. This is their story.

Long before people came to Puerto Rico, hundreds of thousands of parrots flew over the island and the smaller islands nearby. *Iguaca! Iguaca!* the parrots called as they looked for deep nesting holes in the tall trees.

Down below, waves from the Caribbean Sea and the Atlantic Ocean washed the island's white-sand beaches. Delicate orchids and wide-spreading ferns, tiny tree frogs, kapok trees bursting with seedpods, and big, scaly iguanas covered the land.

iguaca (ih-GWAH-kah)

Iguaca! Iguaca! the parrots called as they flew to sierra palm trees to eat their dark, bitter fruit.

Around 5000 BCE, people came to the island in canoes from lands to the south. These people planted corn, yucca, sweet potatoes, peanuts, and pineapples. When they looked up, they saw the bright blue flashes of flight feathers.

More groups of people came. The Taínos arrived around 800 CE. They hunted the parrots for food and kept them as pets. Taínos gave the parrots a name, *iguaca*, after their harsh call. They gave the island a name too: Boriquén.

Taínos (TIE-EE-nohs)
Boriquén (boh-ree-KEN)

Iguaca! Iguaca! the parrots called when hurricane winds blew down the old trees where they had their nests. After the hurricanes passed, the parrots flew through the treetops to find new nesting holes.

Christopher Columbus sailed from Europe to Boriquén in 1493 and claimed the island for Spain. Soon Spanish settlers were planting crops on the island and building houses and schools with wood, bricks, and stone. Each time hurricanes destroyed their homes and schools, the settlers rebuilt them.

The Spaniards called the parrots *cotorras*, and they gave the island a new name: Puerto Rico, "rich port."

cotorras (koh-TOH-rahs)
Puerto Rico (PWAIR-toh REE-koh)

In the treetops, the parrots searched for mates. The new pairs of parrots sat on branches, bowing, calling back and forth to each other, and fluffing their wings and tails. Each pair raised one family of chicks every year.

Now people from many other parts of the world came to live in Puerto Rico. In 1513, Africans were brought to the island to toil as slaves under the hot sun in fields of sugarcane and other crops.

More people came from Spain too, and they married Taínos and Africans. They all called themselves Boricuas, people of Boriquén, but they were still ruled by Spain.

Boricuas (boh-REE-kwahs)

Iguaca! Iguaca! the parrots called when red-tailed hawks chased them in the treetops. The parrots flocked together to protect themselves from the hawks.

For centuries, people from other countries in Europe tried to capture Puerto Rico. These countries wanted to control the deep harbor at San Juan, the capital city, where merchant ships and warships could be launched.

The Boricuas protected their island. Starting in 1539, they built a fort that grew and grew until its walls were 18 feet (5.5 meters) thick. For hundreds of years, no country was able to take Puerto Rico away from Spain.

San Juan (san HWAN)

Iguaca! Iguaca! the parrots called when they found that their nesting holes had been invaded by creatures brought to the island by settlers. Black rats from the settlers' ships climbed the tall trees and ate the parrots' eggs. Honeybees that had escaped from hives swarmed into the parrots' nests.

In 1898, the United States declared war on Spain. The war was really about Cuba, another of Spain's colonies, but the fighting spilled over into Puerto Rico. Thousands of American soldiers landed on the island and began battling Spanish troops. Spain lost the war, and lost control of Puerto Rico. The island became a territory of the United States, and in 1917, Puerto Ricans became US citizens.

Iguaca! Iguaca! the parrots called as the forests where they made their nests were cut down. The parrots began to disappear from places where they had flown for millions of years. By 1937, there were only about two thousand Puerto Rican parrots in the Luquillo Mountains to the east. A few years later, the parrots were living in just one place, El Yunque, a tropical rain forest in those mountains.

After Puerto Ricans gained American citizenship, many of them moved to the United States. Those who stayed in rural parts on the island built houses and farms in the areas where parrots had once lived. Many of the parrots' tall, old trees were made into charcoal to use for cooking fires. And people still hunted and trapped the parrots.

Luquillo (loo-KEE-yoh)
El Yunque (ell YOON-keh)

In the 1950s, birds called pearly-eyed thrashers moved into the rain forest and tried to steal the parrots' nesting holes. Like clever thieves, these birds enter places where other birds are struggling to live and compete with them for nest sites. The parrots fought the thrashers, jabbing at them with their sharp beaks and defending their nests with harsh cries. But the parrots now had too many enemies and too few trees. The flock became smaller and smaller. By 1954, there were only two hundred parrots left.

Puerto Ricans elected their first governor, and the island became a US commonwealth—not a state, not an independent nation, but something in between. The people argued: Should their island remain a commonwealth? Should it be a state? Should it be independent of the United States? Everyone had a different idea, but all were proud to say "*Yo soy Boricua.* I am Puerto Rican."

Yo soy Boricua. (yo soy boh-REEK-wah)

The flock of Puerto Rican parrots became even smaller. By 1967, only twenty-four parrots lived in El Yunque. *Iguaca! Iguaca!* the parrots called as they looked for someplace—any place—to find food and nesting holes for their chicks.

Puerto Ricans looked up and saw that their iguacas were almost gone. People had nearly caused the parrots to become extinct. Now people started to help the parrots stay alive.

In 1968, the governments of the United States and the Commonwealth of Puerto Rico worked together to create the Puerto Rican Parrot Recovery Program. Its goal was to save and protect the parrots. The first part of the plan was to create an aviary, a safe place for parrots to live and raise chicks.

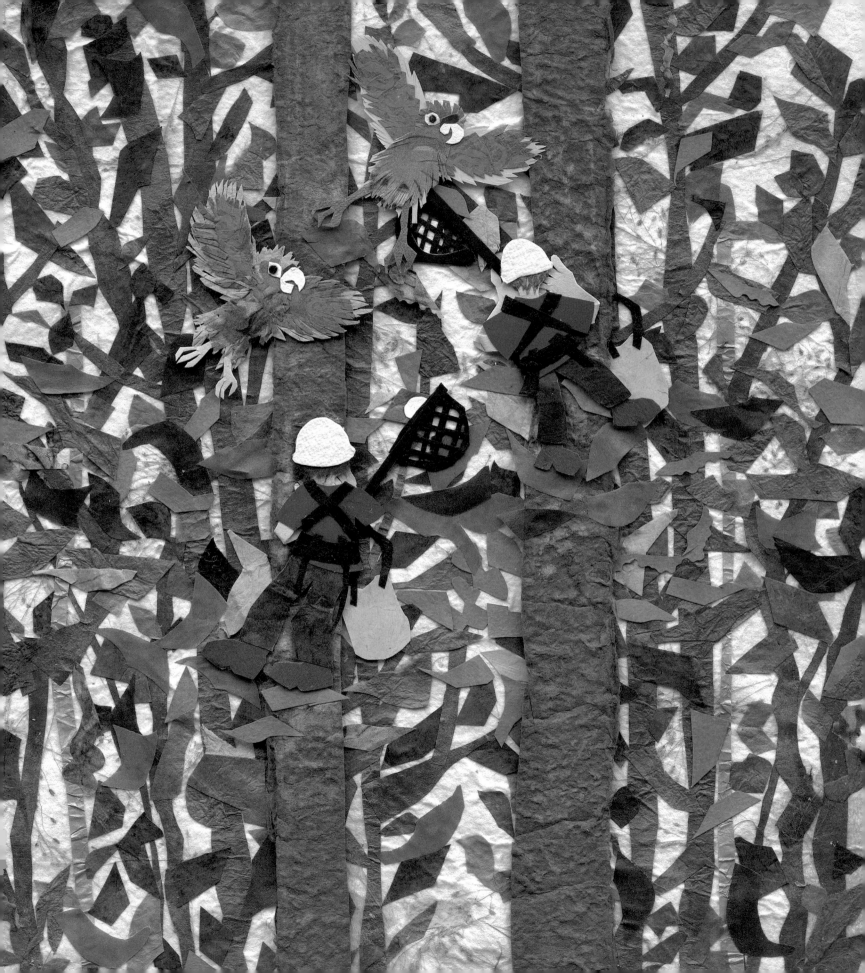

Parrots squawked as scientists with long-handled nets gently lifted eggs and chicks from their nesting holes. The scientists always left at least one egg or chick in each nest so some birds could continue living in the wild.

In 1973, Luquillo Aviary opened in El Yunque. Incubators in the aviary kept the eggs warm. The Puerto Rican parrots raised in captivity had no experience as parents, so Hispaniolan parrots helped raise the chicks. These parrots come from the nearby island of Hispaniola. They are like cousins of Puerto Rican parrots but are not as rare.

 Hispaniolan/Hispaniola (his-pah-NYOH-lahn/his-pah-NYOH-lah)

Once hundreds of thousands of Puerto Rican parrots flew over the island. By 1975, only thirteen parrots were left in the rain forest.

The worried scientists built special nesting boxes and put them in trees in areas where the parrots were likely to nest. The parrots inspected the nesting boxes and then moved in.

These nesting boxes were deep and dark, like the nesting holes Puerto Rican parrots find in the wild. A bird sitting at the top of the box could not see all the way to the bottom. Pearly-eyed thrashers like to see the bottoms of their nests, so the thrashers left the parrots' nesting boxes alone.

Wild parrots squawked as scientists gently placed chicks from the aviary in their nests so the chicks could learn how to live in the wild. In 1979, the very first chick raised in the aviary flapped out of a wild nest into the rain forest.

The scientists worked hard to keep the parrots healthy—both the captive and the wild birds. One chick was rescued from the wild after its wings were badly damaged by gooey slime inside its nest. The scientists rebuilt the baby parrot's wings using old, discarded parrot feathers, pins, and glue. Then they watched the parrot use its new wings to fly for the first time.

By the end of 1979, there were fifteen captive parrots. Most had come from eggs and chicks taken from wild nests to the aviary.

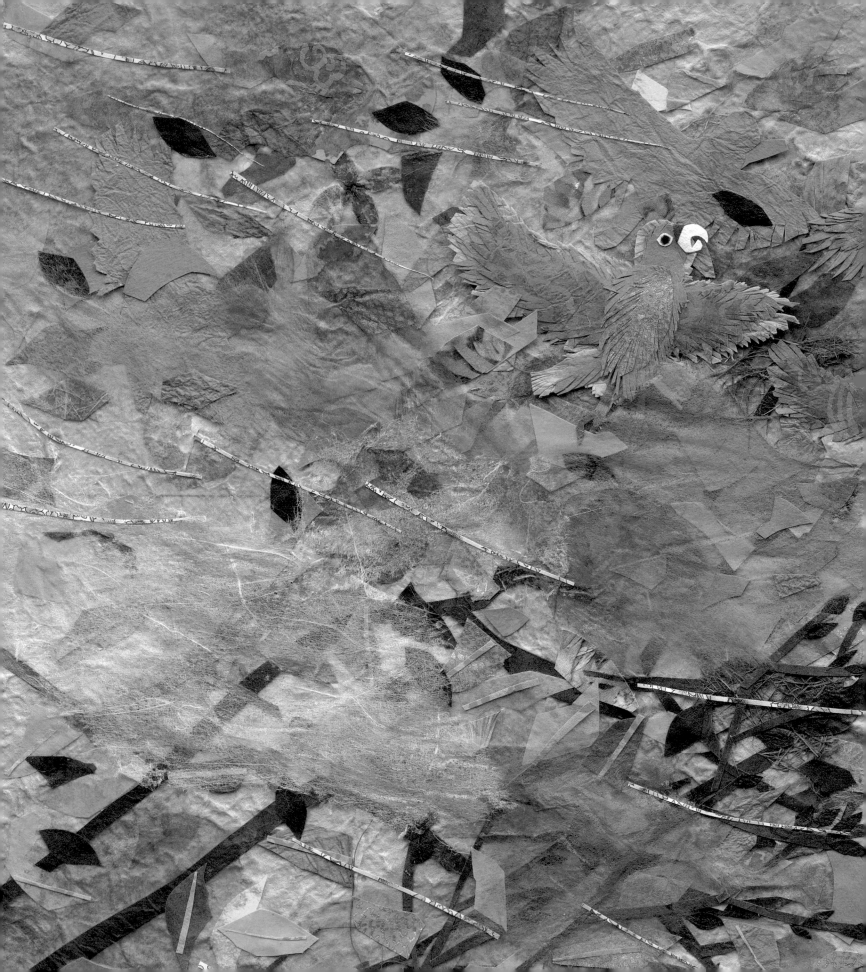

Hurricane Hugo roared through the treetops of Puerto Rico in 1989. *Iguaca! Iguaca!* the parrots called as the winds blew down many of their tall trees.

The hurricane wiped out crops and wrecked buildings and homes. In the aviary, the scientists worried about all the parrots. What if another bad hurricane blew down more trees? What if the aviary was damaged?

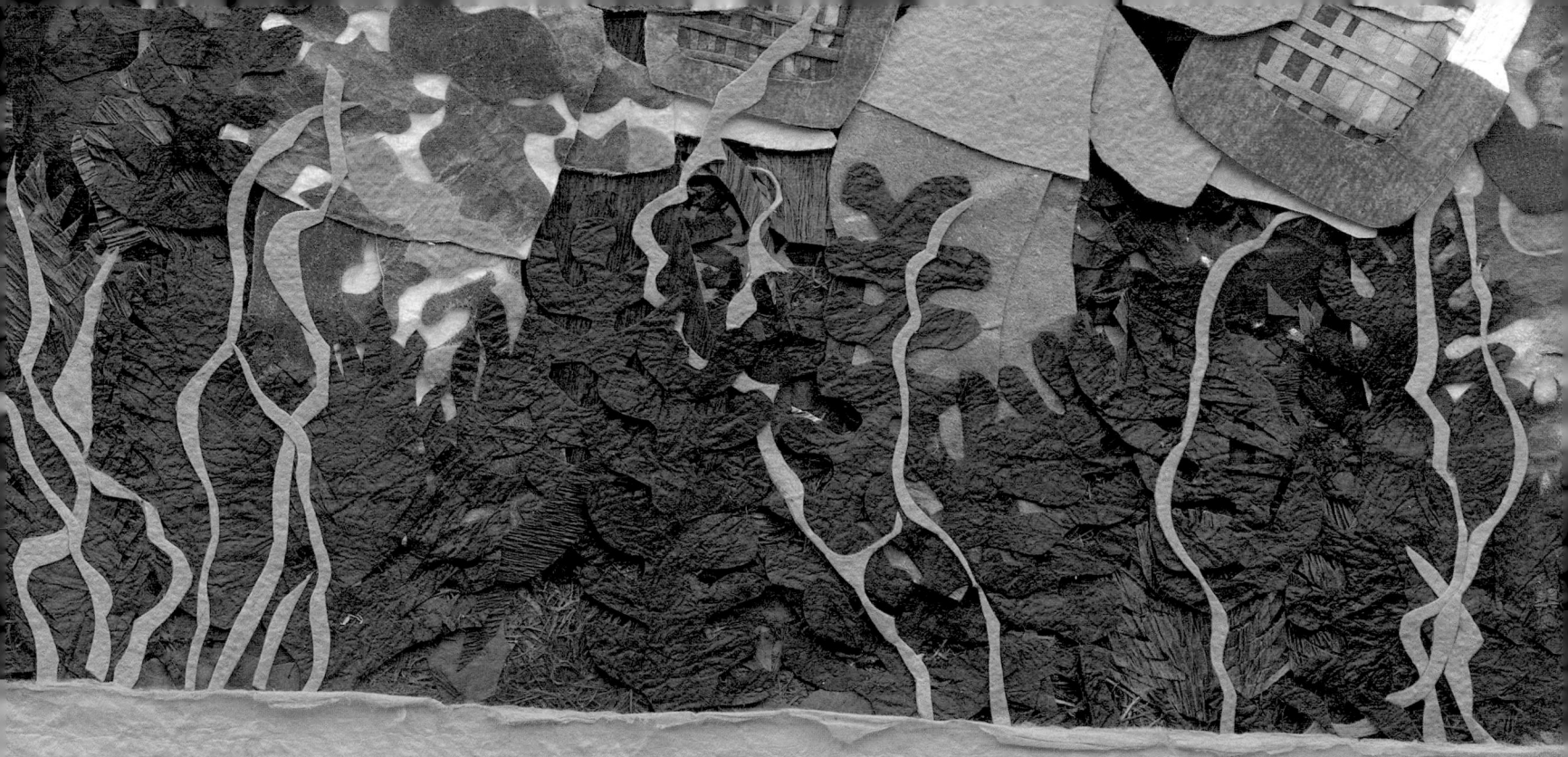

Iguaca! Iguaca! a group of parrots squawked as scientists moved them from Luquillo Aviary to a new aviary in Río Abajo Forest. This forest is less humid than El Yunque, and many parrots had once lived there. Now there were two safe places for captive parrots to live and raise chicks.

Río Abajo Aviary opened in 1993. It had some challenges. Thunderstorms sometimes caused the incubators to lose power. The scientists found generators that kept the power flowing to the incubators.

The scientists also tried some new ideas. They kept more aggressive pairs of parrots away from gentler ones, so the gentler birds would not be frightened. They also caged young parrots with adults, so the birds could see how adult parrots behave. The number of parrots in the aviary grew. By 1999, Río Abajo Aviary had fifty-four Puerto Rican parrots. The recovery program was ready for the next part of its plan: releasing adult parrots raised in captivity into the wild.

Río Abajo (REE-oh ah-BAH-hoh)

In 2000, ten captive-bred parrots were released in El Yunque. It was late spring. The wild chicks had already flown from their nests, and the wild adults were still nearby, where the captive-bred parrots could see them and join them. *Iguaca! Iguaca!* the parrots called as they flew with the newcomers and searched for food.

The captive-bred parrots had been trained to find food and avoid hawks, but many were caught by hawks anyway. So before the next sixteen parrots were released in 2001, they were given extra training. They heard a hawk's whistle as the cutout shape of a hawk was passed over their cages. They watched a trained hawk attack a Hispaniolan parrot that was wearing a protective leather jacket. In time, the parrots learned to stay still or hide if a hawk was nearby. When these parrots were released, more of them survived in the wild.

The scientists were ready to create a second wild flock. In 2006, twenty-two captive-bred parrots were released in Río Abajo Forest. The newly released birds formed pairs, found nesting boxes, and raised their chicks. Dozens of parrots have been released in Río Abajo since then, and they have begun to spread out through the forest.

If you look up from the forest, and you are very lucky, you might catch the bright blue flashes of flight feathers. These are Puerto Rican parrots. They lived on this island for millions of years, and then they nearly vanished from the earth forever. But they are flying over Puerto Rico still, calling, ¡Guaca! ¡Guaca!

Afterword

Wild parrots in flight at El Yunque, blue flight feathers visible

Red-tailed hawk

Puerto Rican parrot

Pearly-eyed thrasher

The Puerto Rican parrot (*Amazona vittata*) is the only parrot native to the United States and its territories. It is a striking bird, about 1 foot (30.5 centimeters) in length, with green feathers, blue flight feathers, a red blaze on its forehead, and wide white rings around its eyes. The parrots give a distinctive bugle, or call, of *Iguaca! Iguaca!* in flight, probably to tell other parrots their direction and speed. Scientists estimate the population was between one hundred thousand and one million birds on the main island of Puerto Rico and the nearby islands of Culebra, Vieques, and Mona in the late fifteenth century, when Christopher Columbus arrived in Puerto Rico.

The history of the parrots is closely linked to the history of Puerto Rico. The parrots' numbers began to shrink in the nineteenth and twentieth centuries as their nesting trees were cut down for logging and farming. Natural enemies including red-tailed hawks, competitors for nesting holes such as pearly-eyed thrashers, the taking of young parrots for pets, and massive hurricanes that devastated the parrots' nesting areas also contributed to their decline. Puerto Rican parrots have been described as one of the ten most endangered birds in the world.

© Ricardo Valentín de la Rosa

Ricardo Valentín de la Rosa, manager of Río Abajo Aviary, checking captive nests; his special hat and vest tell the parrots he is not going to harm their eggs

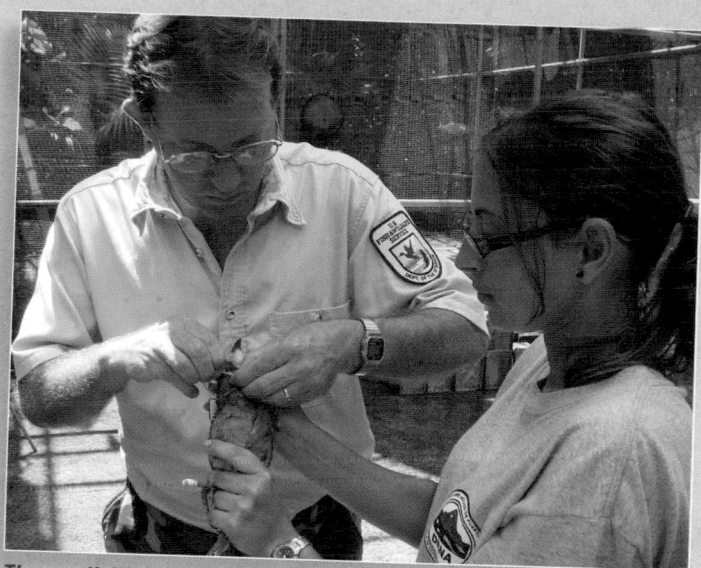

© Ivan Llerandi

Thomas H. White, US Fish & Wildlife Service, and Ana Estrella, Puerto Rico Department of Natural and Environmental Resources, putting ID tag on parrot prior to its release

The Puerto Rican Parrot Recovery Program (PRPRP) is dedicated to conserving, protecting, and managing both wild and captive populations of the parrot so that its status will be changed from endangered to threatened. Begun in 1968, the PRPRP is a cooperative effort between the US Fish & Wildlife Service, the US Forest Service, the Puerto Rico Department of Natural and Environmental Resources, and the US Geological Survey. The goal of the PRPRP is to have self-sufficient wild populations of birds in at least three locations: El Yunque, a rain forest in the Luquillo Mountains; Río Abajo Forest, a drier forest in northwestern Puerto Rico; and a location to be established in the western part of the island by 2016, possibly the rugged Maricao Forest, where abandoned plantations and farms have been reforested over the past sixty years.

© Ricardo Valentín de la Rosa

Released female parrot with transmitter, so it can be tracked, in Río Abajo Forest

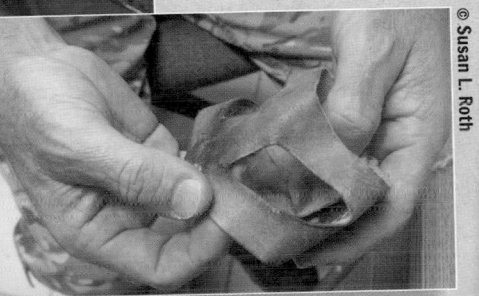

© Susan L. Roth

Leather jacket used to protect Hispaniolan parrot from attack by hawk during predator-aversion training

© Cindy Trumbore

Flight cage at Río Abajo Aviary; fledged chicks live in these cages until their release into the wild

The existence of multiple flocks of parrots has many benefits. Widespread flocks provide a greater chance that the parrots will survive a natural disaster such as a hurricane. Parrots that mate from the different flocks have a wider gene pool and produce chicks with a better chance of survival. And in vast areas such as Río Abajo, a growing population of wild parrots can spread out farther and farther from the aviary site. About a dozen of the birds released from Río Abajo Aviary have relocated to Lake Dos Bocas, three miles from the aviary. Three released birds have been spotted twenty miles away.

Captive parrots at Río Abajo Aviary

Incubator with eggs at Río Abajo Aviary; white eggs are Puerto Rican parrot eggs, and brown eggs are "dummies" that will be slipped into a parrot's nest if eggs must be removed for safety

Chicks from Río Abajo Aviary 2010 captive-breeding season

Wild parrots from 2007 release in Río Abajo Forest; male on right is bowing to the female

Nesting box in tree at Río Abajo Aviary

Pair of parrots at artificial nest in El Yunque

Eggs in captive nesting box, labeled to show destination: to the field, to another aviary, or to foster parents

Survival rates of the parrots grow with each release. Currently there are about 150 birds in each of the two aviaries and between 60 and 95 birds in the wild in El Yunque and Río Abajo Forest combined. The 2013 breeding season is expected to produce a record 100 fledglings in the wild and the two aviaries. Scientists at both aviaries agree that the key to success has been the existence of an established flock of wild birds that can use their vigilance and knowledge of the forest to guide and protect newly released birds. Since 2001, the parrots have nested exclusively in the artificial nesting boxes, but the scientists hope to find parrots in a wild nest one day.

The recovery of the Puerto Rican parrot is a tribute to the passionate and hard-working staff members in the two aviaries. In the words of Ricardo Valentín de la Rosa, who manages Río Abajo Aviary, "I have dedicated my life to saving these extraordinary creatures, which are profoundly emotive, very independent, and a true nightmare to breed in captivity." The scientists' respectful approach to the captive and wild birds is a model for any program dedicated to protecting and managing an endangered species.

Parrot (in carrier) ready for release into El Yunque

Wild Puerto Rican parrot at night

Important Dates in the History of Puerto Rico and Puerto Rican Parrots

c. 5000 BCE: First people arrive in Puerto Rico from South America

c. 2000 BCE: People from Central America arrive

c. 800 CE: Arawak people from South America travel to Puerto Rico; they become known as Taínos

1493: Christopher Columbus lands on Puerto Rico on second journey to the West Indies

1508: Juan Ponce de León founds a settlement in Puerto Rico; island's first school is built

1513: First Africans arrive in Puerto Rico; Spanish government gives settlers permission to marry Taínos

1528: French soldiers attack many Puerto Rican settlements; capital city, San Juan, survives

1539: Construction begins on Fort San Felipe del Morro and continues for four hundred years

1595: British navy tries to capture Puerto Rico and fails

1598: British navy attacks and holds Puerto Rico for several months but flees when plague breaks out among its troops

1625: Dutch troops attack San Juan and are defeated by Spanish soldiers

1702: British soldiers attack city of Arecibo without success

1797: After Spain and France declare war on England, British troops invade Puerto Rico; Puerto Rican volunteers and Spanish soldiers fight off attack of thousands of British troops

1868: In city of Lares, group of Puerto Ricans rebel against Spanish rule; rebellion is planned by Dr. Ramón Emeterio Betances with troops led by Manuel Rojas

1873: Slavery abolished in Puerto Rico

c. 1890: Flocks of 50 to 200 parrots seen throughout northwestern Puerto Rico, including Río Abajo Forest

1898: Spain loses War of 1898; gives Puerto Rico to the United States

1917: Puerto Ricans become citizens of the United States

1935: In Luquillo Mountains, US Forest Service begins program of cutting down trees considered inferior for timber; many palo colorado trees, the most important nesting trees for Puerto Rican parrots, are removed

1937: US Forest Service employees estimate number of Puerto Rican parrots in Puerto Rico at 2000 birds

1940: Parrots found only in El Yunque National Forest

1948: Luis Muñoz Marín becomes first elected governor of Puerto Rico

1952: Puerto Rico becomes United States commonwealth

1954: About 200 Puerto Rican parrots counted in El Yunque

c. 1950s: Pearly-eyed thrashers, nearly unknown in El Yunque until this time, spread into forest and compete with Puerto Rican parrots for nesting sites

1967: About 24 Puerto Rican parrots remain in Puerto Rico; Puerto Rican parrot classified as an endangered species

1968: Puerto Rican Parrot Recovery Program (PRPRP) formed, dedicated to studying and saving the birds

1970: PRPRP begins captive-breeding program in Luquillo Mountains

1973: Luquillo Aviary opens in El Yunque

1975: Only 13 Puerto Rican parrots left in the wild

1976: PRPRP begins putting artificial nesting boxes in trees for the parrots

1979: Luquillo Aviary has 15 captive birds; first captive-bred Puerto Rican parrot chick flies from its nest in the wild

1989: Hurricane Hugo devastates Puerto Rico, knocking down many trees bearing fruit, flowers, and leaves that make up the parrots' diet; only 22 parrots survive in the wild

1993: First group of Puerto Rican parrots transferred to new aviary in Río Abajo Forest

1994: First breeding season in Río Abajo Aviary produces 2 Puerto Rican parrot fledglings, or young birds

1999: Río Abajo Aviary has population of 54 Puerto Rican parrots

2000: First 10 captive-bred Puerto Rican parrots released from Luquillo Aviary into El Yunque

2001: Another 16 Puerto Rican parrots, trained to find food in the wild and avoid predators, released into El Yunque

2002: Another 9 captive-bred Puerto Rican parrots released into El Yunque; total of 144 captive birds now live in the two aviaries

2006: First 22 Puerto Rican parrots, fitted with radio transmitters so they can be tracked, released into Río Abajo Forest; Río Abajo Aviary produces 29 fledglings in one season, a turning point because, with more fledglings produced than released, the program becomes self-sustaining

(continued on next page)

2007: Upgraded Luquillo Aviary, now called US Fish & Wildlife Service (USFWS) Iguaca Aviary, opens in Luquillo forest; includes hurricane room to protect parrots in case of storms

2008: More Puerto Rican parrots released into Río Abajo Forest; 2 active nests seen there

2012: Río Abajo Aviary has 10 breeding pairs of Puerto Rican parrots in the wild; between 60 and 95 wild birds live in the two forests and about 150 captive birds live in each aviary

Puerto Ricans show support in nonbinding referendum to change Puerto Rico's status, expressing preference to become the fifty-first US state, but many reasons make

it unlikely the island's status will change in the near future

2013: Total number of fledglings in the wild and the two aviaries expected to exceed 100, a record for the program

2020: PRPRP objective is to have Puerto Rican parrots downlisted from endangered to threatened status by this date

Authors' Sources

"Amazona vittata." The IUCN Red List of Threatened Species, 2012. http://www.iucnredlist.org/apps/redlist/details/106001666/0.

Breining, Greg. "A Fighting Chance: The Puerto Rican Parrot Makes a Comeback." *Audubon* (September-October 2009): 91-95.

Fox, Ben. "Endangered Puerto Rican Parrot on the Rise." Associated Press, June 25, 2011.

Kirkpatrick, Randy. "The Decline, Recovery, and Captive Management Potential of the Puerto Rican Parrot." *Proceedings of the 1994 Annual Conference of the Southeast Association of Fish and Wildlife Agencies* 48: 401-410.

Moores, Charlie. "The Puerto Rican Parrot." *Talking Naturally* (blog), January 4, 2009. http://www.talking-naturally.co.uk/puerto-rican-parrot/.

"Prehistory of the Caribbean Culture Area." National Park Service. http://www.nps.gov/seac/caribpre.htm.

"Puerto Rican Amazon *Amazona vittata*." BirdLife International (2012) Species fact sheet. June 10, 2012. http://www.birdlife.org/datazone/speciesfactsheet.php?id=1666.

"Puerto Rican Parrot." Audubon.org: Audubon WatchList. http://audubon2.org/watchlist/viewSpecies.jsp?id=168.

"Puerto Rican Parrot." U.S. Fish & Wildlife Service. http://www.fws.gov/southeast/prparrot/pdf/PR_parrot_FS.pdf.

"Puerto Rican Parrot Project (Río Abajo aviary)." Chirping Central. http://chirpingcentral.site-ym.com/?page=puerto_ricanricargeo.

Snyder, Noel F. R., James W. Wiley, and Cameron B. Kepler. *The Parrots of Luquillo: Natural History and Conservation of the Puerto Rican Parrot.* Los Angeles, CA: Western Foundation of Vertebrate Zoology, 1987.

Stafford, Dr. Mark L. "The Crown Jewel of Puerto Rico." Parrots International. http://www.parrotsinternational.org/Species_Pages/Puerto_Rican_Amazon_pages/PR_Parrot_status_page.htm.

Stille, Darlene R. *Puerto Rico.* Danbury, CT: Children's Press, 2009.

Valentín de la Rosa, Ricardo. "Conservation: The Puerto Rican Parrot at the Río Abajo Aviary." *Parrot Life* 4 (2007): 10-13.

———. "La cotorra de Puerto Rico Amazona vittata vittata Boddaert 1783 en el carso." (abstract). *Focus* 4, no. 2 (2005): 39-46.

———. Personal interview with the authors. Río Abajo Forest, Puerto Rico: June 19, 2012.

Wagenheim, Kal, and Olga Jiménez de Wagenheim, eds. *The Puerto Ricans: A Documentary History.* Princeton, NJ: Markus Wiener Publications, 2008.

"Welcome to Puerto Rico! History." http://www.topuertorico.org/history.

White, Thomas H. Jr., Jaime A. Collazo, and Francisco J. Villela. "Survival of Captive-Reared Parrots Released in the Caribbean National Forest." *The Condor* 107 (2005): 424-432.

———, and Fernando Nunez-Garcia. "From Cage to Rainforest." *Endangered Species Bulletin* 28, no. 4 (July-December 2003): 16.

———. Personal interview with the authors. Río Grande, Puerto Rico: June 18, 2012.

Acknowledgments

Special thanks to Thomas H. White Jr., Wildlife Biologist, US Fish and Wildlife Service, and Ricardo Valentín de la Rosa, Manager, Río Abajo Aviary, for their critiques of the text, the generous gift of their time during interviews, and the photographs they provided; and to all the staff of Río Abajo Aviary for an unforgettable glimpse of Puerto Rican parrots in flight. Our sincere thanks go to Olga Jiménez de Wagenheim, Professor Emerita in History, Rutgers University, and Kal Wagenheim, editor of Caribbean UPDATE, for their critical reading of the historical information and their helpful comments. S.L.R. also wishes to thank Olga Guartan, Nancy Patz, Jasmin Rubero, JAAAHLE, and MP for their support.

LEE & LOW BOOKS Inc., 95 Madison Avenue, New York, NY 10016, leeandlow.com
Manufactured in China by Jade Productions, January 2014
Book design by Christy Hale   Book production by The Kids at Our House
The text is set in Francois One   The illustrations are rendered in paper and fabric collage
10 9 8 7 6 5 4 3 2
First Edition
Library of Congress Cataloging-in-Publication Data
Roth, Susan L.
Parrots over Puerto Rico / by Susan L. Roth and Cindy Trumbore ; collages by Susan L. Roth. — First edition.
pages cm. — (Parrots)
Summary: "A combined history of the Puerto Rican parrot and the island of Puerto Rico, highlighting current efforts to save the Puerto Rican parrot by protecting and managing this endangered species"—Provided by publisher. Includes bibliographical references.
ISBN 978-1-62014-004-8 (hardcover : alkaline paper)
1. Puerto Rican parrot—Juvenile literature. 2. Puerto Rican parrot—Conservation—Juvenile literature. 3. Endangered species—Puerto Rico—Juvenile literature. 4. Natural history—Puerto Rico—Juvenile literature. 5. Puerto Rico—Environmental conditions—Juvenile literature. I. Trumbore, Cindy. II. Title.
QL696.P7R68 2013   597.7097295—dc23   2012048195